The Secrets of High Growth Businesses

By Susan Banfield & Martin Ellis

Copyright Susan Banfield & Martin Ellis

The authors have asserted their rights under the Copyright, Designs and Patents Act 1988 to be identified as the authors of this work.

All rights reserved. Without limiting the rights under copyright reserved above, no part of this publication may be reproduced, stored or introduced into a retrieval system or transmitted, in any form or by means (electronic, mechanical, photocopying, recording or otherwise), without the prior written permission of both the copyright owner and the publisher of this book.

Published by: www.b2bgrowth.co.uk

Contents

Contents 2

About The Authors 3

Introduction 4

Shift One... Ditch The Rose Tinted Glasses 8

Shift Two... Shift Your Business Paradigm 13

Shift Three... Better Understand Your Market Opportunity 18

Shift Four... 'Lead The Business', Don't 'Be The Business' 23

Shift Five... Strategise Not Fantasise 29

Shift Six... Innovate To Dominate 34

Shift Seven... Make Marketing Matter 39

Shift Eight... Feel The Fear And Sell Like You Mean It 44

Shift Nine... Plan, Prepare And Behave Like Winners 50

Implementing The 9 High Growth Shifts 55

In Conclusion 58

About The Authors

Let us introduce ourselves so that you know we have the knowledge, experience and credibility to share **'The Secrets of High Growth Businesses'** with you. Between the two of us we have over 40 years of Business Growth coaching, training and consulting.

We have now worked with well over a 1,000 businesses on Business Growth projects. These businesses have ranged from start-ups to multi-nationals but have mostly been established small and medium sized companies.

Because we have worked with so many businesses trading in so many different markets we have been able to study, analyse and learn the true differences between those companies that are successful in achieving High Growth and those that aren't.

Susan Banfield & Martin Ellis

Introduction

We are going to take you through a structured approach for transforming your business into one capable of achieving consistently high levels of sales and profit growth.

We are going to share with you '**The 9 High Growth Shifts**' that you and your business can make in order to transform your business into one capable of achieving consistently higher levels of profitable growth.

This approach isn't for everyone, but it is for you if you are an ambitious Business Leader operating in Business to Business markets.

It is definitely for you if you are running an established business with unexploited growth potential or if you are struggling to break out of a static or slow sales cycle.

Finally, and very importantly, it is only for you if you and your business are ready, willing and able to become a High Growth Business.

'The 9 High Growth Shifts' will place you not only in control of your sales growth, but also of the underlying business organisation required to support and sustain that high growth.

By using these 9 Shifts you will build your business into being a formidable competitor.

But, let be clear, this approach isn't about 'Sales Tips', although, of course, we do cover the sales process in some detail.

It's about how to grow your whole business into being a more significant and substantial player in your chosen market place. About how to build a market leading, market focused organisation, capable of achieving its true potential, and how you can ultimately maximise, multiply and realise the full net worth of your business.

We are going to take you through a really practical step by step strategy for you to create your own High Growth Business.

Let's look at some of the business challenges that we are going to try and help you work on.

Do any of these sound like your business?

- ☐ Are you struggling to achieve consistent levels of sustainable profitable growth?
- ☐ Is the 'hand of fate' controlling your sales growth and not you?
- ☐ Do you badly need more sales prospects, or do you have good prospects but are struggling to get in front of them to present your case?
- ☐ Maybe you feel that your marketing is ineffective, and that there is no connection between how much you spend and what you get back?
- ☐ Are you perhaps worried that your business is missing out on the whole Digital Marketing phenomenon?
- ☐ Do your sales people seem to be struggling to close those vital sales that you badly need?
- ☐ Does your website feel as if it is lost somewhere in cyberspace and hardly anybody ever goes there?
- ☐ Perhaps you feel your competitors are doing much better than you?

- Maybe you think that business is not what it used to be but you are not really sure why?

So if these are the sorts of things that are going on in your business, how does that make you feel?

- Do you sometimes think "I'm doing lots of good things", but why isn't it working?
- Do you feel you are struggling to keep lots of different balls in the air and are frightened of dropping one?
- Do you feel the business is over dependent on you?
- Everybody brings everything to you. It's all down to you to make it happen?
- Do you feel you are in need of new ideas, inspiration?
- Are you perhaps genuinely worried about what the future holds?
- Are you questioning your own leadership skills?
- Do you wonder if you are somehow missing a vital piece of the jigsaw?
- Does it feel like there is an invisible ceiling on your revenue, on your growth and on your profits that you just simply can't find a way of breaking through?

If any of these ring any bells with you, then you are in the right place.

So what is the real problem when businesses are struggling for growth?

Well, the first thing we are going to say is there is no invisible glass ceiling on your business. Of course your business is capable of High Growth.

But, in order to achieve that you need to understand, to adopt and to implement the practices and behaviours of High Growth Businesses.

Using our experience and analysis of working with many hundreds of High Growth Businesses we have distilled this down to what we now call 'The 9 High Growth Shifts'.

We are sharing these with you so you can use them in your business and implement them.

The great thing is, once you have made these 9 Shifts, you actually realise that the glass ceiling on your business growth was never actually there.

You will be able to push through and achieve the levels of revenue and profit growth that you never previously considered were achievable.

You will do all of this whilst you and your team will enjoy the benefits that come from working in a successful growing and profitable business.

Shift One...
Ditch The Rose Tinted Glasses

So, the first vital Shift, is to take a reality check right now.

That's right, a long hard objective look at your business.

Its internal strengths and weaknesses, and the market place opportunities and threats.

It's a core characteristic of High Growth companies that they undertake very regular detailed reviews.

This is because the faster a business grows, the faster the rate of change in the business, and therefore the greater the risk of either not spotting problems or missing opportunities.

Because let's be very clear about one very important thing.

If your business is struggling for growth, there will be at least one, and probably many more obstacles to growth that you need to fix.

One of the self-assessment tools we regularly use with management teams is called the **"MASC Mapper™"**.

This simple tool identifies the degree of cohesion or disparity between managers about their perception of the business's internal strengths, weaknesses and external opportunities and threats.

It might surprise you just how often we see major differences of opinion between people who are supposedly working as a team to develop their business.

> **Only recently the Managing Director of a £4m industrial products manufacturing company placed his head in his hands after reading his MASC Mapper™ report and said;**
> *"I simply cannot believe we are so far apart as a management team in our thinking, it's like we work for different companies".*

'The 9 High Growth Shifts' give you the key areas against which you need to benchmark your business during your review.

Using these 9 Shifts you can identify where you are already strong and where you need to implement and fix to create new strengths.

So right now would be a good time to reach for your pen and paper so you can start the process of review as we go through 'The 9 High Growth Shifts'.

As you read about each individual Shift, score yourself between 1 and 10.

If the Shift is one you have already made and are doing already to a consistently high standard, then that's great give yourself a high score 8, 9, 10.

If it's a Shift you are doing but you are still on your way to making it fully effective then score 4, 5, 6, or 7.

If it's a Shift you have yet to start to make or are just starting out on, then score 1, 2, or 3.

So by the end of this book you will already have a clear view where you are on your High Growth journey and the actions you need to take so you can start to behave increasingly more and more like a High Growth business.

Remember, and this is important, you shouldn't pick and choose which Shifts you make – you should plan to make all 9 in order to achieve High Growth.

It's very hard to be completely objective about our own businesses, we are after all the architects who created them and it's not always easy to stand back and be critical.

But this Review isn't just about finding your weaknesses, but also about identifying and building on your strengths.

Your business may have lots of hidden strengths it needs to capitalise on, and this review needs to highlight those too.

Your review should look both internally at your business and also externally at your market place.

It is after all the combination of these that will dictate your future.

The internal review has to include looking very closely at you, your Management Team and staff too.

You have to question if collectively you as a team have the knowledge and skills to make the right decisions for your business and the ability to implement them effectively.

The external market review needs to make sure you have a clear understanding of the market place in which you are trading.

To evaluate if you fully understand both the market opportunities and the threats your business needs to address as it looks for growth.

We cover this in more detail in Shift 3.

The fact is, to be able to plan your journey towards High Growth, you first need to know where you are starting from.

Without this initial honest appraisal, you risk trying to make 'The 9 High Growth Shifts' under false assumptions about what really needs to change.

So the key High Growth Actions from this First Shift are to:

- STOP and Remove your rose tinted glasses.
- Take quality time to take stock.
- Review everything objectively and honestly against the 9 Shifts, starting with this one.

We strongly suggest that you now reach for a pen and score yourself as honestly and objectively as you can after each Shift.

Score: SHIFT ONE: Ditch The Rose Tinted Glasses

1	2	3	4	5	6	7	8	9	10
STARTING OUT			ON OUR WAY>>>>				DOING IT		

Shift Two…
Shift Your Business Paradigm

So what do we mean by 'Business Paradigm'?

A business paradigm is the set of assumptions, concepts, values, and practices that constitutes a particular way of viewing reality for the organisation that shares them.

In other words it is the way that you and your business perceive yourselves and the business world within which you operate.

It is therefore what drives your business and what actually influences your decision making and the way your business works on a day to day basis.

It dictates the way in which you do things, what you prioritise and see as important, and it is a key part of your business's culture.

So let's take a quick look at the most common business paradigms that we see:

- **Technology & Design-Led Paradigm** – these businesses are focused inward on R&D, technical innovation and developing new products and intellectual property.
- **Manufacturing or Operations-Led Paradigm** – the core purpose of these businesses is to become Better at Production, on Reducing Cost and Time, & Improving Quality.
- **Sales-Led Paradigm** – this is where the core purpose of the business is to sell what it has on the shelf regardless if it's right for customers.
- **Profit-Led Paradigm** – the core purpose of these businesses is to make large profits regardless of how. The business is focused on generating cash and profit.

- **Visionary-Led Paradigm** – occasionally businesses are driven to solve an unsolved problem, to invent radically new products or solutions or to be very different.
- **Competitor-Led Paradigm** – these businesses takes their lead from other companies and simply copy what others do rather than doing something new.

And last but by no means least;

- **Market-Led Business Paradigm** – here the core purpose of the business is to satisfy customer needs, wants and expectations and build mutually beneficial customer relationships.

Oh, and one we will cover later under leadership ….the **'It's All About 'ME' Paradigm'** – you can guess what drives those businesses.

> For example we worked with a £7m high tech electronic instrumentation design and manufacture company who were totally R&D and Manufacturing Led. As a result only 1 in 4 of their new products ever recovered the R&D & production investment and went on to make a profit.
>
> This was simply because they were focused on technical innovation rather than on what customers actually wanted. Under our guidance they made a Market-Led paradigm shift which dramatically improved the new product success rate to 100% and within 3 years had increased the company net worth by 7 times.

Now many of these different Business Paradigms can often be seen to be successful, and some companies are a mix of two or three.

But what we consistently see in High Growth Businesses is a Market-Led Paradigm taking a dominant role in determining what the business does and who it does it for.

The Market-Led Paradigm ensures the business uses customer, competitor and market intelligence to find (or create) and seize profitable market opportunities.

It ensures the business maintains a detailed knowledge and understanding of its customers, competitors and the overall market place in which it operates.

The Market Led Paradigm works for one simple reason:

- All businesses are dependent on having customers.

Adopting a Market-Led Paradigm is the best way of finding, winning and keeping them.

A truly Market-Led business will also give you a distinct competitive advantage over your competitors as most won't be.

The important questions you need to ask yourself:

- "Is being a genuinely Market-Led business one of your major business paradigms?"
- Is your business truly driven by its market or is it more driven by your own personal preferences, or those of your Managers, or your Shareholders and Stakeholders

We see a lot of dysfunctional non market-led business paradigms in low growth businesses.

So the key High Growth Actions from Shift Two are to:

- To take an honest look at the paradigms operating in your business.
- To ask yourself if the forces that are dictating how your business operates are truly about those for satisfying customer needs.

If your business isn't truly Market-Led you will undoubtedly be making poor decisions and missing important opportunities so you will want to make this important Shift.

Score: SHIFT TWO: Shift Your Business Paradigm

1	2	3	4	5	6	7	8	9	10
STARTING OUT			ON OUR WAY>>>>				DOING IT		

Shift Three…
Better Understand Your Market Opportunity

This is one of the Shifts that we feel that we shouldn't really have to refer to.

But it's a Shift which we know the vast majority of low growth businesses still need to make.

It's about having sufficient accurate, up to date market intelligence upon which to make the key decisions in your business.

The sad fact is the vast majority of low growth businesses don't undertake the extensive market research and analysis that they need to in order to understand what their market opportunity really is and how to capture it.

Did you know that the UK market research industry is worth £3bn per annum and employs 60,000 people? Probably not.

But how much of that £3bn came from your business last year?

If you think market research is only for big businesses, you should think again. Ask yourself:

- How many important decisions do you make about your business without having the supporting market intelligence?
- How many new products or services have you launched?
- How many prices have you set?
- How many marketing campaigns have you run?
- How many decisions have you taken without having first investigated fully the related customer perceptions and competitive positioning implications?

So few SMEs invest in market research it's one of the real defining differences between low and High Growth Businesses.

Market research enables you to make important decisions and base strategies for growth on facts rather than assumptions.

> One start up business in the telecommunications industry that we worked with was a new entrant to the market place. They found it very difficult to win good sized orders against well-established competitors.
>
> As a result they were mainly being used for top up orders or if a current supplier let them down. The Managing Director, on our advice, took it upon himself to actively go out to visit many of the potential customers.
>
> Not to sell to them but in a market research role to find out about their needs and expectations and how best he could move his business into being a first line supplier. As a result he was able to find a number of gaps in their competitors' armoury which presented an opportunity for them to fill.
>
> By listening to these customers he was not only able to return with a revised customer proposition, but he was able to build relationships and trust amongst these customers because he had shown he cared about knowing what the customers really wanted and not just offered a standard solution.
>
> This hands on approach taken by the Managing Director has resulted in much more business coming their way and given them the opportunity to demonstrate their expertise, leading to significantly more contracts being won and a trebling of turnover.

So why don't SME businesses invest in research?

Well complacency is a big one, people thinking they already know all they need to know. That is almost never true.

Another common mistake is to assume that your sales people are bringing back all the market intelligence needed. In our experience sales people make very poor market researchers. They lack objectivity and impartiality and customers tend to treat their questioning with some caution.

And of course 'cost' is the big barrier. Market research can be expensive.

But you have to ask yourself, what has the true cost of making poor decisions been to your business over the years? Where would your business be now if it had been making better ones?

Our experience shows very clearly the link between businesses investing in market research and High Growth. Market intelligence gives you the power to make the right decisions.

The secret to business success does not come from staring at your P&L and balance sheet. Nor by sitting around your board room table wondering where the sales are coming from next year.

The task of you as a Business Leader is to invest time, energy and resources to fully understand the market opportunity you are targeting.

So your High Growth Actions are quite simple:

- Look at your business and ask yourself how much do you really know about your target market opportunity?

- How much of that knowledge is based on researched evidence versus guesswork and assumption?
- Are you still making key decisions without the market intelligence to back them up?

If so, then things need to change.

Score: SHIFT THREE: Better Understand Your Market Opportunity

1	2	3	4	5	6	7	8	9	10
STARTING OUT			ON OUR WAY>>>>				DOING IT		

Shift Four…
'Lead The Business', Don't 'Be The Business'

This is about that knotty topic – Leadership.

The simple fact is;

> **"Most businesses stop growing when they reach the limitations of their leaders."**

Yes, what we are saying is that your business is only ever likely to achieve a level of growth that you as its leader are capable of taking it to.

That's a scary thought for some.

We can all blame our customers, our competitors, the government or the global economy for our growth problems. But the bottom line is it's the decisions we make as Business Leaders that ultimately determines how our business will perform.

There is a huge amount written and discussed about Leadership, you could fill a library with it. But in our experience what we see in businesses who are struggling for growth or who have plateaued is that they are at the limit of their leadership capability.

This is typically characterised by:

- Know it all owners and bosses whose vision revolves entirely around what they want to get out of their business for themselves.
- Leaders whose egos are threatened by the thought of having anyone else senior in the business who might challenge them or has greater skills than they have.
- They see themselves as 'the business'.

- Their 'not invented here' philosophy kills the ideas and aspirations of others in the business.
- They micro manage everything and everybody, and can only delegate work to others but not the responsibility and authority to go with it.
- They are somewhat risk averse, fearful of losing what they already have, and unwilling to spend the time and energy to mitigate risk preferring to go with 'gut feel'.
- They rarely seek outside investment nor are they willing to share ownership. They would rather have 100% of nothing than 50% of something.

Perhaps the most memorable example we had of this with a client was also a hugely disappointing one, and proves the old adage that *'you can lead a horse to water, but you can't make it drink'*.

This 30 year trading £3m business had been slamming itself into a glass ceiling of its own making for many years. The Managing Director is a 100% shareholder and had all of the characteristics just described, and was very much a 'control freak' and workaholic.

The net result was that for many years he had created a highly profitable small business, but as his competitors grew he failed to grow with them and they gained significantly from economies of scale he couldn't. The business stagnated and profits fell into losses. He simply ran out of answers as to how to grow his business.

In all fairness, he did take a lot advice and paid to have growth plans drawn up, he even took the initiative to bring in some new senior management blood. But sadly he himself couldn't manage to change his old ways, he quickly disposed of the new management and their new ideas and the business continues to bump along the bottom of the cookie jar simply eking out an existence.

By contrast the five core attributes we consistently see in High Growth Business Leaders, and that you should seek to emulate in yours, are:

Firstly – to have an absolute clarity about the target market opportunity your business is intending to capitalise on.

Be knowledgeable, passionate and highly motivated by this opportunity and bring this enthusiasm and determination for it into your business.

Secondly – to have a clear vision of precisely how that market opportunity can be captured by your business.

To visualise what the results of that success will look like and state them in terms of a vision with clear business goals and objectives.

Ensuring your vision is for the whole business and for all of its stakeholders to benefit from, not just you.

Thirdly – to build a winning team around you. You can't go it alone.

Find people with the higher skills your growing business will need. Recruit for the business you want to be not the one you are today.

Invest in finding the best people, but don't carry dead wood and act quickly to resolve people issues.

Fourthly – develop the ability and willingness to delegate authority and responsibility to others and to release the reins.

Set clear objectives and strategies and give your team the freedom to get on and make them happen.

Finally – be prepared to take risks, but take the time and energy to research and make them calculated risks.

Don't see failure as a reason for not doing something again, but as a learning curve.

Be confident enough to invest in the future of your business and be able to convince others to make an investment too.

So, in order to create your High Growth Business, then you as the Business Leader must first have these necessary skills and attributes to be able to lead a High Growth Business.

The fact is, most people running successful High Growth Businesses aren't actually born able to do that, but they have taken the time and energy required to gain those skills.

They have invested in their education, training and coaching.

They have experimented and learned from their mistakes.

They surround themselves with other highly capable people, and they seek the advice and counselling of others.

Making this transition from 'being the business' to 'leading the business' is a tough one for many smaller business owners.

We understand that, but where there is a will there is a way.

So, the key High Growth Actions from this Shift are:

- Think about the two different descriptions of Business Leaders we have just given you, the low growth and the High Growth.
- Decide where you are today and what needs to change.
- Create your own 'Personal Leadership Development plan' and
- Develop your own leadership skills towards those needed to be a High Growth leader.

Score: SHIFT FOUR: 'Lead The Business', Don't 'Be The Business'

1	2	3	4	5	6	7	8	9	10
STARTING OUT			ON OUR WAY>>>>				DOING IT		

Shift Five…

Strategise Not Fantasise

You might be interested to know that about 90% of the low growth businesses we have worked with over the years really don't have clear strategies for how they will achieve growth.

There is no point in fantasising about High Growth if you haven't really worked out the strategies for how you are going to achieve it.

Because that's exactly what a Strategy is – the HOW. That's why you need them.

There are 2 basic types of Strategy.

Competitive Strategies and Optimisation Strategies.

Competitive Strategies are without doubt the ones that could drive the greatest growth in your business.

But they are invariably difficult to create, and the one that we find lots and lots of low growth companies really struggle with and don't have.

Competitive strategies relate to the aspects of your business that makes it truly unique and gives you a competitive edge when you're marketing & selling to customers. You may think of them as **Unique Selling Propositions**. Ideally they should be capable of being protected and from being copied by your competitors.

The trouble is creating something genuinely unique that customers want and competitors can't match or copy seems almost impossible for many businesses. Typical examples of competitive strategies are: patented products or sole licensed products, protectable intellectual property, formulas, recipes, processes and so on.

The one unique thing all companies have is their name, their brand. But trying to get a small business brand established in a large market is very hard.

One of the traps that many smaller businesses fall into, is operating in too large a target market. They don't use market segmentation and market positioning techniques to try to find a smaller part of the market they could make their own. A niche in which they could build a substantial market share and become a recognised brand and be the 'go to business' for that sector.

> A great example of this is a client in the automotive supply chain. Five years ago this was a start-up company with no significant capital who chose to operate in a market dominated by huge international players servicing the major brands of the global automotive industry.
>
> How could they possibly do that?
>
> Well they spotted a niche opportunity, not new products, just an innovative new way of supplying those products which met a very specific need, this formed a competitive strategy that it turns out not only avoided the huge competitors, but in fact enlisted their support in promoting them.
>
> They will shortly hit £5m turnover and are making an excellent ROI. They are a Tier 1 supplier now to dozens of major car and truck manufacturers and are exporting all over the world.
>
> They have become the 'go to business' for their specialist services.

Optimisation Strategies by contrast are strategies for doing the many things that both you and your competitors have to do.

There is nothing really unique about them and you can easily copy what others are doing just as they can copy you.

These are your strategies for activities like accounting, logistics, customer service, IT, marketing, sales, recruitment, warehousing, production, purchasing and so on.

The critical thing about Optimisation Strategies is 'continuous improvement', the need to get better all the time.

In this regard both you and your competitors are running the same race.

Sometimes you may be in the lead, sometimes they may lead.

For example you might make a stepped change in your operational capability.

You go out and buy the very latest machine that works twice as fast as the machine that you had before and which your competitors don't have.

That's great, in the short maybe even medium term you gain a genuine competitive advantage over your competitors.

But....that is until your competitors then buys the next generation of new machine after yours, and they move ahead of you.

Optimisation strategies are a never ending game of catch up that you have no choice other than to play.

Quite often we are only talking about marginal gains, talking about moving forward in small increments, getting better a bit at a time, continuous improvement in all these areas.

Sometimes you can make innovative breakthroughs and achieve major step changes.

The key with Optimisation Strategies is to remember the old adage 'the whole is greater than the sum of the parts'.

Lots of small improvements can add up to make a big overall difference.

So the key High Growth Action as far as Strategise not Fantasise is concerned is to review your current strategies:

- Firstly to see if you have a genuine Competitive Strategy and if not could you create one.
- Secondly look to see if you are really capitalising on your Optimisation Strategies and finding at least that extra few percent across everything you do.

Score: SHIFT FIVE: Strategise Not Fantasise

1	2	3	4	5	6	7	8	9	10
STARTING OUT			ON OUR WAY>>>>				DOING IT		

Shift Six…

Innovate To Dominate

So what is Innovation?

Innovation is all about challenging the status quo and looking to do things differently and better in your business.

It could be to make something quicker, cheaper, better quality, more attractive, easier, more functional, look better, more competitive or to be of course completely new.

Really anything, however big or small, to be an improvement on what is there already. Whether your processes, products, services, staff, systems, resources, it's just challenging everything and trying to do things differently to achieve better results.

But why bother? 'If it ain't broke don't fix it' you may say.

Well to quote Henry Ford 'If you always do what you've always done, you'll always get what you've always got'.

That is true in engineering terms, but it's often far from true in business? The fact is doing the same old thing as we always did in business usually gets us less, often a lot less. The world moves on and we have to move with it.

Economic growth is pretty much stagnating both domestically and globally. So for most businesses sales growth will have to come from taking business from their competitors.

Innovation is the driving force behind a business's ability to be consistently competitive and to stay ahead of the competition.

A recent Barclay's survey showed that those businesses achieving High Growth are those focused on innovation. Those who enhance their existing products and services continuously and regularly launch new ones.

High Growth Businesses are entering new markets, new geographic territories and are taking the fight to their competitors by being innovative.

According to various studies the top 20% of all businesses achieve on average 38% of revenues from new products launched within the last 3 years.

How does your business stack up against that High Growth criteria?

There are many ways you can innovate, but they all need one thing – a business culture that supports, promotes and rewards innovation.

It never ceases to amaze us how much untapped talent sits within the staff of most businesses.

How little time some business leaders take to encourage staff to be innovative in their jobs.

These are the 6 most common characteristics we see in High Growth Businesses regarding their approach to innovation:

One – They involve their customers, their suppliers, their distributors and other stakeholders in their business. They don't assume they know all the answers. User-Driven Innovation is becoming a key technique being used by many High Growth Businesses.

Two - When they hire new people they look for those with a different perspective to existing employees so they will bring new ideas and challenge the status quo.

Three – They don't financially reward innovation – they make it an expected key part of everyone's job, they set targets for new ideas and include a review of the individual's innovations in their appraisals.

Four – They have ditched their suggestion box – and build time into everyone's diary to spend time on innovation and they encourage working in cross functional teams.

Five – They borrow innovation from other industries – they watch the very best at work and see if you can learn from them.

Six – They set challenges for innovation – they identify where the biggest benefits for innovation will come from and prioritise those with clear objectives.

Innovation should become a key part of the culture of your business.

A culture that promotes looking at ways of doing everything better at every level in every job.

Getting your whole workforce thinking and challenging the status quo.

> We recently worked with a £2m marketing agency whose annual customer satisfaction survey strongly indicated that customers would like them to extend their services into digital communications.
>
> However, the market research also indicated this was because of customer dissatisfaction with other suppliers and the need for a new innovative approach to be taken in the provision of digital services.
>
> The management team were tasked with looking at the main competition and to determine their weaknesses from a customer's perspective.
>
> They then used this knowledge to develop an innovative new way of pricing and delivering digital services which when test marketed to customers really seemed to hit the spot.
>
> This resulted in a whole new specialist digital marketing agency being set up which in its first year is on route to a £1m turnover and is extending their client base from which the core business's sales growth is also benefitting.

So the key High Growth Action for this Shift is to ask yourself:

- Does my business truly have a culture of innovation?
- Am I taking positive steps to engage all the stakeholders in the business to drive and stimulate innovation

If the answer is no, then you need to start to make this Shift using the 5 High Growth characteristics we outlined as a starting point.

Score: SHIFT SIX: Innovate To Dominate

1	2	3	4	5	6	7	8	9	10
STARTING OUT			ON OUR WAY>>>>				DOING IT		

Shift Seven...
Make Marketing Matter

Did you know that **"My Marketing Isn't Working"** is the most common reason given by small and medium sized businesses for why they are struggling to achieve higher levels of sustained business growth?

But why is that and what are the common underlying problems?

We see 7 common problems in low growth companies:

Problem 1: Limited Marketing Scope.

Most low growth businesses see marketing as just the promotional and visible aspects: such as what visitors see on your Website, adverts, press releases, emails, catalogues etc. They don't apply marketing well in its strategic, research or market-led organisational role.

Problem 2: Copying Other Companies.

Many businesses are heavily influenced by other companies' promotional activity. They copy it rather than finding their own solution. Standing out for something important in the minds of our target customers is what matters not looking like everyone else.

Problem 3: Lack of Customer Input.

A failure to obtain objective customer feedback about their marketing, or to obtain customer input before they invest in new marketing materials and campaigns.

Problem 4: Ignorance is Bliss.

Marketing is not a core skill of most SMEs, so there is a great lack of knowledge about it in many low growth businesses.

Problem 5: Self-Centred Focus

Businesses focus on providing lots of information about their company, what they do, how they do it. There is a massive absence of customer related content to show empathy and understanding. Marketing should always be focused on the customer and helping them to solve their problems and challenges.

Problem 6: No Marketing Budget

A large number of SMEs simply don't have a budget for marketing or anywhere near big enough budget for marketing. Marketing is treated as a 'nice to have' not a 'need to have' activity and expenditure on marketing is minimised.

Problem 7: Poor Marketing Execution

Many SMEs are very poor at implementing their marketing activity. They mail out to inaccurate databases, their Websites are out of date, their blogs and news pages are full of old content.

They repeat old messages and have nothing new, current or interesting to say.

Marketing is done in an ad-hoc and inconsistent way, with no regular ongoing communication with customers. It simply fails to take any real priority in the business.

So if these are the mistakes we see low growth businesses making, then it follows that the opposite is what we see High Growth Businesses doing:

- They are market-led and embrace marketing in all its facets.

- They do their own thing and don't try to copy others.

- They obtain customer input into their marketing and monitor customer feedback.

- They obtain a high level of marketing skills or use those of expert 3rd party providers.

- They produce marketing content from a customers' perspective.

- They have a marketing budget – typically at least 5% of revenue.

- They take marketing seriously and consistently, marketing week in and week out and treat this as a high priority.

- They do not turn their marketing tap on and off. They keep it running at full blast.

- They implement marketing like the business they want to be not what they are.

In a nutshell they believe and act like marketing really matters.

A good example of this is a client of ours who really decided to make marketing matter.

This £3m company in the forestry machinery industry has really embraced marketing to such an extent that its brand has become synonymous with the specialist products it sells in its target market.

They have achieved this simply by investing in their brand and in their marketing.

The company spends around 5% of its turnover on marketing which crosses all media from trade advertising, exhibitions and PR to website, social media and email marketing. So much so that their biggest problem right now is coping with the high level of interest this activity generates. A nice problem to have.

The key to their marketing success is quality and consistency – they don't overwhelm customers with junk, rather they keep them well informed about things they know they are interested in with high quality written and visual content on a monthly basis. Their web traffic & SEO, their email open and click through rates, their YouTube views and their exhibition enquiry rates exceed all norms for this reason.

So key High Growth Action from this Shift is simple:

- Make Marketing far more important, far better resourced and central to your business growth.

Score: SHIFT SEVEN: Make Marketing Matter

1	2	3	4	5	6	7	8	9	10
STARTING OUT			ON OUR WAY>>>>				DOING IT		

Shift Eight…
Feel The Fear And Sell Like You Mean It

Ralph Waldo Emerson once said "Build a better mousetrap and the world will beat a path to your door".

There is some truth in that, and High Growth Businesses are indeed often those who have built the better mouse traps. They have created products and services that do their job brilliantly and those customers' need and want to buy.

However, if you have a great mouse trap that nobody knows about, well they can hardly beat a path to your door to buy it can they?

We have already covered the need to make marketing matter in your business, that's how customers get to know about your mouse trap and how to find the path to your door. Indeed in some cases maybe to buy it too.

But in many B2B businesses, marketing only finds the opportunity and creates awareness, it doesn't make the sale.

That's where you need to start selling.

Selling is the art of enabling customers to see the benefits of investing in your products or services and convincing them to buy them.

> **"It's a strange thing, but we often find that 'Selling' seems like a dirty word in some low growth businesses."**

A real reluctance to engage customers in a dialogue that will result in a sale.

But why so?

The simple answer is fear and a lack of confidence.

What we see in High Growth Businesses is confidence in 5 different ways:

Confidence One: that your target customer actually really needs and wants a product or service like yours.

Confidence Two: that your specific product or service is genuinely the best choice for your customer to make.

Confidence Three: to pick up the phone and call customers or to fix that appointment.

Confidence Four: to be able to make customers see the benefits of investing in your products and services over those of your competitors.

Confidence Five: the confidence to convince customers to buy from you, and to ask for and take the order.

You want all these 5 confidences in your businesses in order to be good at selling.

You want confidence in what you are offering and your ability to offer it. It is really vital for your business to have a grip of these 5 confidences and the ability to make sales.

It is not just about having good sales people either.

Selling should be something everybody in the business can contribute to.

Many of the staff in your business have an opportunity to interact with customers at different customer touch points along the customer journey.

Make everyone confident to sell at every point.

In B2B selling, customers very rarely buy things they don't need.

So the very fact you are targeting them should mean you already know they are a qualified potential customer. That's why you do your market research.

You just have to convince them of the benefits of your products or services over those of your competitors.

You have to get your head round the fact that you are trying to help your customers to make a good decision for their business, not selling them something they don't need or want.

You want to give them the knowledge and information to make the right decisions to buy from you in order to help them solve their problems or take their opportunities.

"Ditch any stigma around selling, feel the fear and make your business a selling machine."

Once you have the 5 confidences you need to become good at selling, you need to have an effective sales process.

Most low growth businesses are really poor at staying in contact with and capitalising on selling opportunities with their existing customers, let alone their prospects. With their existing customers they miss opportunities to increase penetration and their share of customer spend or to cross sell to other parts of the same business or to seek referrals into their customers' network. With prospects they give up too easily. They fail to stay in contact and to keep selling.

Do you realise that most sales are not made until at least after the fifth sales contact? But most businesses stop making sales contacts after 2 or 3! This simple fact alone could give you a huge advantage over your competitors by becoming the business that does stay in contact and makes those extra calls and visits.

Low growth businesses are often pretty appalling at capturing information, sharing & using intelligence about customers. They either don't have or don't use properly a good Customer Relationship Management system.

Selling needs to be a part of what your business does, sales are what everyone in your business needs to understand and to have the confidence to make.

A good example of this is a £1m PR company we worked with who has now taken the whole 'Sell Like You Mean It" approach to heart.

Following a 'Ditch The Rose Tinted Glasses' internal review, they quickly realised that whilst all of the members of the team had opportunities to sell when they made contact with clients or prospects, that only some of the team were making sales calls, and finding and winning sales opportunities.

With an investment in some sales training and coaching, and a little encouragement and incentivisation, all of the team are now capable and willing to make sales calls to follow up the direct mail campaigns.

These conversations have led to a significant increase in sales as all the members of the team now have a chance to give useful advice and information and find out the problems clients have that they need help addressing.

So the key High Growth Actions from this Shift are to:

- Review where you are now in terms of the 5 confidences
- Review your sales culture and your sales processes and systems and to start to 'Feel The Fear And Sell Like You Mean It'.

Score: **SHIFT EIGHT: Feel The Fear And Sell Like You Mean It**

1	2	3	4	5	6	7	8	9	10
STARTING OUT			ON OUR WAY>>>>				DOING IT		

Shift Nine…
Plan, Prepare And Behave like Winners

Here is the Final Shift

Those in the know tell us that only 50% of small businesses have a Business Plan. By which of course they mean the types of Business Plans that are full of wish lists and financial projections. These plans are typically produced to keep the bank or shareholders happy. Then more often than not they are placed firmly in a drawer somewhere and forgotten about.

Hardly any business we see, High or low growth uses these types of Business Plans as anything more than a historic reference.

So do High Growth Businesses have plans, if so what sort?

Well there are a few truths in old sayings like "time spent in planning is seldom wasted" and "starting a journey without a plan is like firing a gun without aiming". So yes in order to achieve High Growth you need a plan. But what sort of plan?

Well we believe a good Business Plan, should be a working plan that is a living, breathing document that you actually use to run your business.

A source of inspiration, and guidance to you and your team that sets out the narrative, the story about your proposed business journey.

Your plan wants to read like a good book with a beginning, a middle and an end. The more riveting and exciting the story, the more likely it will engage you and your team in successfully implementing it.

We must tell you this lovely story about business planning. Some years ago we helped a £2m training company develop a new growth strategy and Business Plan. It was a very ambitious plan in an over supplied market.

The plan was to double sales over 3 years to £4m and to generate a 10% ROS profit. The business was very task oriented and liked detailed plans to follow so they set about ticking things off as fast as they could.

We heard next to nothing from them for just over 2 years when we got a phone call.

"*We've done it*" said the CEO……. "*Sorry, you've done what?*" we said ……."*Implemented and finished the plan a year early*" he said.

And they had. They had made a major paradigm shift, explored and entered new markets, created a unique market position and new competitive strategy, innovated their training offer and marketed and sold like it really mattered. They had not only doubled sales but were approaching a 20% ROS.

"*So how can we help you*" we asked, "*We need our next 3 year plan*" said the CEO.

You should tell your business story in Four Chapters, each covering where you are now, what will change over the duration of the plan and where you will end up:

Chapter One is your **Market Opportunity** – a clear description of your target market opportunity.

What is happening in your market place, who your customers will be going forward, who your competitors will be and where you plan to fit in to the market.

Chapter Two covers your **Ambitions** regarding that market opportunity, in terms of your vision of the benefits for everyone in the future if you succeed, your objectives and goals along the journey.

Chapter Three: covers your **Strategies** for achieving your ambitions with the target market opportunity both competitive and optimisation.

Chapter Four covers the **Capabilities** the business will need to implement the strategies, to achieve the ambitions and capture the market opportunity. The people, processes, resources etc.

These four chapters create the narrative to your business growth.

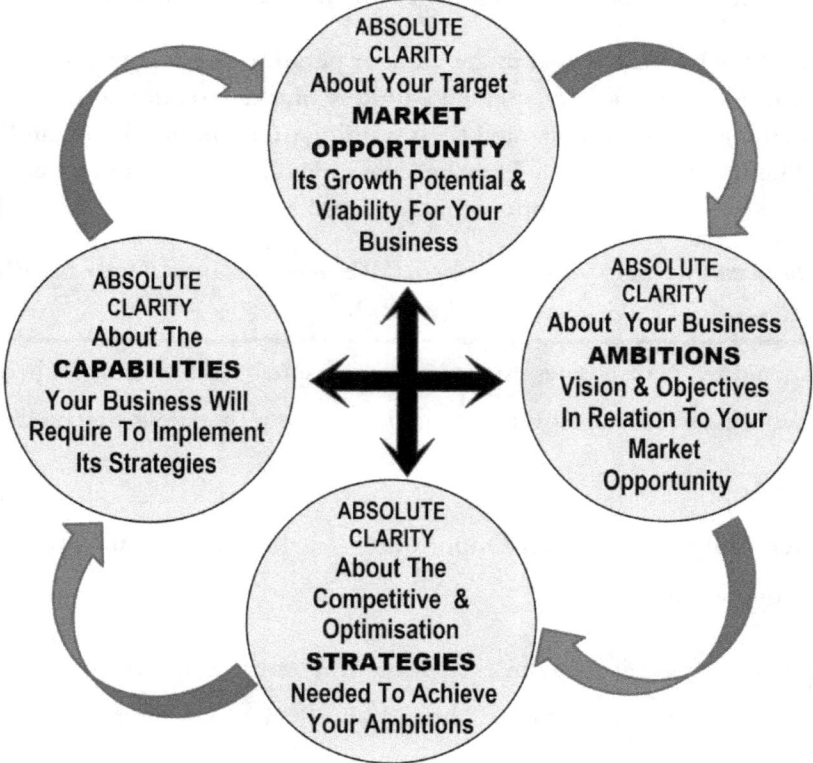

You will then need to add Four Appendices:

Appendix One is a Critical Success Factors Action Plan – focused on the first 12 months of the plan. It's the list of the make or break actions and outcomes that will determine if the business will be on course for hitting its short and longer term objectives.

Appendix Two is your Sales & Marketing Communications Plan – a 12 month detailed plan of the key activities that will be taken on a month by month basis.

Appendix Three is your Investment Plan – showing where, when and how key investments will be made.

Appendix Four are your Financial projections & budget – the next 12 months shown monthly and then quarterly up to 3 years ahead.

Ensuring that each Critical Success Factor and the Marketing Plan are properly budgeted for or else they won't happen!

That's it – your High Growth Business Plan. Four chapters and four appendices. No more no less.

So your key High Growth Action for this Shift is simple:

- Write it, share it, refer to it, update it.... Believe in it.

Score: **SHIFT NINE: Plan, Prepare And Behave like Winners**

1	2	3	4	5	6	7	8	9	10
STARTING OUT			**ON OUR WAY>>>>**				**DOING IT**		

Implementing The 9 High Growth Shifts

OK so that was the last of the 9 Shifts that your business needs to make in order to become High Growth.

How did you score your business – all 10 out of 10's, or 1's out of 10 or somewhere between?

The fact is, a bit like pieces in a jigsaw all of these Shifts need to be made to complete the picture.

You must aspire to do all of them really well, and to do them, and improve on them, on an ongoing and continuous basis.

So, we promised you a Step by Step Strategy for creating a High Growth Business and that is making 'The 9 High Growth Shifts'.

Making these 9 Shifts will enable you to:

- ✓ Have control over your revenue and profit growth.
- ✓ Have robust underlying processes in place for finding and winning new customers.
- ✓ Generate new customers on demand, putting you in control of your revenue growth.
- ✓ Retain and enjoy the full potential of your existing customers.

We also promised you a process by which you can maximise your selling prices and retain higher profits.

How you can build a market leading, market focused team capable of achieving your expectations.

How you can maximise, multiply and realise the full net worth of your business.

We believe we have shown you that too.

We did all that by telling you that you needed to make these 9 Shifts:

1. To **Ditch The Rose Tinted Glasses** and take a long hard reality check.
2. To **Shift Your Business Paradigm** and to adopt a Market Led Paradigm.
3. To **Better Understand Your Market Opportunity** and understand your marketplace far better than you do now.
4. To **'Lead The Business', Don't 'Be The Business'**, for you to become a High Growth Business Leader.
5. To **Strategise Not Fantasise** and create Competitive and Optimisation winning formulas for growth.
6. To **Innovate To Dominate** and dare to be different and to be better at everything.
7. To **Make Marketing Matter** and place it absolutely at the core of everything your business does.
8. To **Feel The Fear And Sell Like You Mean It** so your business becomes a mean selling machine.
9. To **Plan, Prepare and Behave Like Winners** so you and your team know where you are going and how you are going to get there.

In Conclusion

So what should be your next steps to High Growth?

Well, you have a choice to make, an important choice about the future of your business. Your choice in many ways is quite simple.

You can either choose to take positive actions, change your situation and to move your business forward. Or, you can choose to stay as you are and just hope that things will get better.

But we would caution you.

Standing by and doing nothing when a problem occurs is very rarely the right choice in life or in business. Of course, just what actions you choose to take are entirely down to you. It is your business, you're the Business Leader, you are in charge.

So in conclusion, perhaps now is a good time for you to ask yourself a simple question…..

- **Which you would prefer…..**

To carry on running your business as it currently is, perhaps not really sure about what the future may hold……

- **Or…….**

To take positive action and to begin your own High Growth journey today. Learn from The Secrets of High Growth Businesses and implement 'The 9 High Growth Shifts' ……. starting right now.

It's now entirely up to you.

We wish you the very best of luck with your High Growth journey. Our website is full of additional Business Growth content and should you require any help we have a range of services you can access.

If you would like to discuss your Business Growth challenges please contact us.

www.b2bgrowth.co.uk

www.ingramcontent.com/pod-product-compliance
Lightning Source LLC
Chambersburg PA
CBHW072247170526
45158CB00003BA/1021